At the Lake
by PJ Dietz

At American Reading Company, we believe that reading success is the cornerstone of society-wide successes, both large and small. We believe the way to open a child to the possibilities of the world is through the power of books. To that end, our goal is to enable children to read—independently—for an hour each day. We are a resource to help schools and teachers accomplish that goal swiftly and effectively.

Our most notable program, 100 Book Challenge, is our own proprietary independent reading program that has helped schools all over the country dramatically improve reading scores among their students, regardless of reading level.

Book design by Nupur Shah

First Edition, February 2006
ISBN 1-59301-446-5

Copyright © 2006 by American Reading Company™

All rights reserved.
Published in the United States by American Reading Company.

AMERICAN READING COMPANY
Independence. One book at a time.

www.americanreading.com

At the Lake

At the lake, we saw the wave.

At the lake, we saw the duck.

At the lake, we saw the rocks.

At the lake, we saw the tree.

At the lake, we saw the bike.

At the lake, we saw the canoe.

At the lake, we saw the trash can.

At the lake, we saw the boat.

At the lake, we saw the city.

At the lake, we saw the **sunset**.

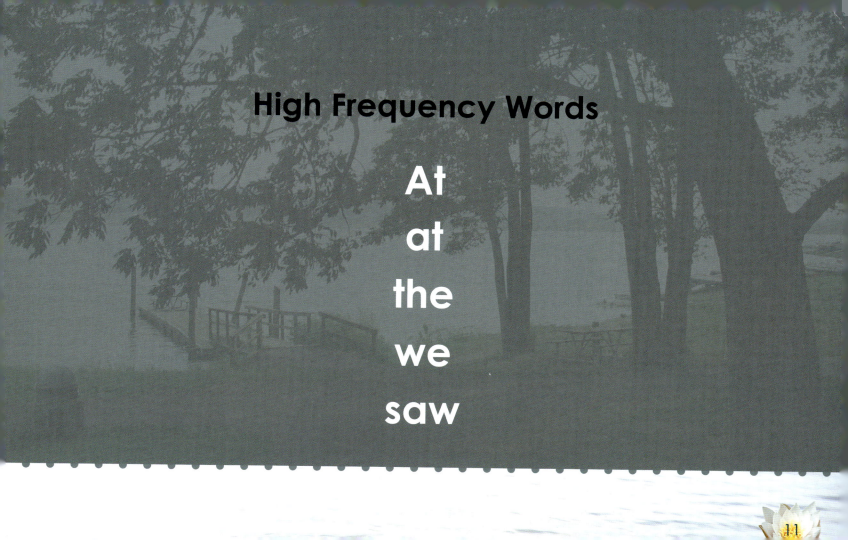

High Frequency Words

At
at
the
we
saw

YY: Skills Card

Reader _____ Room _____

Strategies

	Date:		
Listen to the title and first page.			
Use the title and first page to figure out the rest of the pages.			
Use my finger to point to each word as I read.			
Use the picture and the first letter to figure out the words.			
Use the spaces to separate words.			
Tell someone what the book was about.			
Read at home every night.			

I can get my mouth ready for

b	c	d	f
g	h	j	k
l	m	n	p
r	s	t	z

I can read these words

I	love	a	cat
is	The	the	A
stop	Stop	go	Cat

© 2006 by American Reading Company™

Can you match the words to the pictures?

tree

city

duck

rocks

wave